£3

CW00796400

GRASSHOPPER

HEART

Also by Andrew Lansdown

Poetry
HOMECOMING
COUNTERPOISE
WINDFALLS
WAKING AND ALWAYS
A BALL OF GOLD (children's poetry)

Non-fiction
BLATANT AND PROUD

Short Fiction
THE BOWGADA BIRDS

THE
GRASSHOPPER
HEART

Andrew Lansdown

A division of HarperCollins*Publishers*

Arts for Australians
Australia Council

Collins/Angus & Robertson Publishers'
creative writing programme is assisted
by the Australia Council, the Australian
government's arts advisory and support organisation.

AN ANGUS & ROBERTSON BOOK

First published in Australia in 1991 by
Collins/Angus & Robertson Publishers Australia

Collins/Angus & Robertson Publishers Australia
A division of HarperCollins Publishers (Aust) Pty Ltd
Unit 4, Eden Park, 31 Waterloo Road, North Ryde
NSW 2113, Australia

William Collins Publishers Ltd
31 View Road, Glenfield, Auckland 10, New Zealand

Angus & Robertson (UK)
16 Golden Square, London W1R 4BN, United Kingdom

National Library of Australia
Cataloguing-in-Publication data:

Lansdown, Andrew, 1954–
   The grasshopper heart.

   ISBN 0 207 17027 4.

   I. Title.

A821.3

Typeset in Australia by Midland Typesetters
Printed in Australia by Australian Print Group
Cover painting: Angling Club by Robert Hagan
Courtesy Art Nouveau Publishing Co Pty Ltd

5 4 3 2 1
95 94 93 92 91

For Iain and Liz Parker

ACKNOWLEDGEMENTS

Poems in this collection (some in slightly different form) have previously appeared in the *Adelaide Review*, the *Age*, the *Australian*, *Anthology of Australian Religious Poetry* (Collins Dove, 1986), *Family Matters*, *Fremantle Arts Review*, *Island*, *Linq*, Mattara Prize Anthologies *Properties of the Poet* and *Pictures From an Exhibition* (University of Newcastle, 1987 and 1989), *Northern Perspective*, *Overland*, *Phoenix Review*, *Poetry Australia*, *Quadrant*, *Southerly*, *Southern Review*, *Studio*, *Verse* (Scotland), the *Weekend Australia*, the *West Australian*, *Westerly* and *Wordhord: A Critical Selection of Contemporary Western Australian Poetry* (Fremantle Arts Centre Press, 1989). Some poems have been broadcast on 'A First Hearing' (Australian Broadcasting Corporation) and 'Writers' Radio' (Radio 5UV, University of Adelaide). The author gratefully acknowledges financial assistance from the Literature Board of the Australia Council.

For you shall go out with joy,
and be led forth with peace:
the mountains and the hills shall break forth
before you into singing,
and all the trees shall clap their hands.

Isaiah, lv:xii

CONTENTS

Pine and Poem

Unlike other trees, the Norfolk Island pine
neither gives up and droops over nor disperses
into branches. No weeping, no compromise.

It surges straight up. Even its laterals
support the single perpendicular.
Each ring of branches is a set of guys

anchored to the sky to keep the centre post
poised. Diminishing in diameter,
the spoked strata shape a tent

as a farthingale shapes a dress.
The green frame, tall, conical, waiting
to be covered. Trim the sky for a canvas.

Peg it down. Don't let it flap loose
from your imagination. Gales are gathering.
Strong winds are coming. Stake out

your tent. Enter in. Enter in to the calm.

Windmill

The windmill is a dandelion
on a tall stem. Behold, above
the yellow-petalled paddock,
an inflorescence of iron.

The stalk is a lattice-work,
a high scaffolding,
upholding the enormous bloom.
Dusky wood swallows lurk

along the laterals, face
each other in their Zorro masks.
A wagtail swings like a vane.
The wind gathers pace.

A sheoak by the dam
shifts in her skirts,
curtsies to the drifting duck,
the drinking lamb.

The metal corolla begins to hum.
It whirrs and whirls
as if flicked from its stem
by an invisible thumb.

Child with Melon
(Naomi, nearly one)

Stepping into the kitchen
I see my daughter
sitting in the highchair
eating water-melon,

her pale face eclipsed
by the red half-moon,
her soft fists round
the sharp, green rind,

her blonde hair tangled
in the ripe flesh.
Oh child! Glancing up,
she smiles, a pip

slipping from her chin.

Feigning Sleep

(Naomi, nearly two)

'Daddy, night,' she says, patting my leg.
She takes my thumb, whose circumference
is almost as great as her grip, and tugs
at me to follow. And of course I must

leave my work and go with her to the far
wall where she sits and insists I do
the same. As soon as I'm seated she stands
to sit again on my outstretched legs,

her back on my belly, her head on my chest.
I spread her cardigan—it is, it occurs
to me, hardly larger than a handkerchief—
over her shoulders as is the ritual.

'Night,' I say. She sighs, snuggles down,
pretends the absent sun has pulled her
into blackness. Lord, this brightness!
A child caped with a cardigan in my lap.

My daughter. Then suddenly afraid that sleep
might really sneak up and snatch her off,
she hops up and wanders away. No longer
needed, I go back, not to the poem

in progress, but to a new poem, this poem,
as a man who has been blessed returns
to his business but cannot resume
business-as-usual, being unsettled by calm.

In Her Haste
(Naomi, nearly three)

She is going out with her mother
and she is calling, 'Goodbye Dad!' And
she is pushing open the fly-wire door,
always wanting to be off or anxious not

to be left behind. 'Bye Daddy!'
she bellows, bursting with importance
and impatience. From my desk
I call, 'See you later!' and hear,

thinly from the distance of the driveway,
her sweet, unsought rejoinder, 'See you
later! Don't forget the toilet paper!'
These impish pleasures, heightened by im-

perfections. I smile like an alligator.

Pines

These pines, or the seeds of their parents,
were imported from America.
Planted in Australia, they are perturbed
by memories of the Northern Hemisphere.

See that tree, for instance—the tuft
of dead needles caught in the crook
of branch and trunk. It is the throat-tassel
of a moose—the bell of a big bull.

Look. Many trees have grown beards.
The uppermost branches of some are bare—
all bone and peeling velvet.
They are restless in the rough wind.

Listen. Farther off in the forest,
the clash of antlers!

Palm

The cotton palm. This is it. Don't ask
for more. It's on the Swan River foreshore,
is ten metres tall, has a trunk like the leg
of a pachyderm, has a topknot of green fan-fronds
below which grey leaf-limbs lie overlapping
along the trunk, thick and smooth
as thatching—flattened against the trunk,
head down like dozing bats. But forget
about that. Consider this. Help me create it.

The palm is a great and splendid rooster.
The living leaves are his unruly comb,
the flattened fronds are his neck-feathers.
Imagine that—the green comb, the grey cowl
of the palm-tree-cock. Now see at the base
of the smoothed-down nape, a few feathers
are ruffled, sticking up—as if the rooster
were raising his hackles, being heckled
by the windy crowing of a rival cock.

Oak, Oakover Homestead

The oak (grant me this
conceit) is a herd
of elephants. They are
all in there, the pachyderms,
packed in that pillar
of wood and piled
upon one another's
shoulders. Those higher up
are snorkelling out
their trunks—enormous trunks
stretching out
and dropping down
to sweep along
the grass-sweet ground.
Look at them,
the English-oak-elephants,
snuffling about for acorns!

Oak, Jacoby Park

The oak is a hen—a pullet
plumped up with green plumage.
The oak-hen: exotic,
enormous—not to mention

economical. Before moulting
each autumn, it lays
numerous eggs—hard-boiled,
served up in egg-cups.

The Brobdingnagian Banana

The banana tree is
a Brobdingnagian brick-layer.
He has suspended an enormous

plumb-bob from a green rope
to read the lean of things,
to plot the perpendicular. There is

a beauty in this, too—a unity
of utility and artistry,
a melding of function and form.

For the plumb-bob is made
of beaten-copper bracts
layered within each other—

large leaf-sheets
cupped curving and diminishing
to a core of nothing. And

between each sheet (observe
how the top one is loosened)
there is a row of golden trumpets

summoning the swift honeyeaters,
those feathered Lilliputians,
with a fanfare of nectar.

Wattle, Mundaring Weir

The wattle tree was once a battleship.
The mainmast, the cut of the sail,
the sound of the sea when the wind
is up—these many confirmations.
But most telling of all, the hammocks
slung haphazardly from the bark's
rigging. Pleasing, really, to ponder
the seedy crew snug in their bedding,
dreaming of piracies and plunder.
Given germination, each crew will
captain his own land-locked wattleship,
bombard spring with bursts of blossom.

White Water

The unblemished water
at the river's bend
comes suddenly upon
a reef of rocks,
runs on ruffed with foam.

The rocks are a rookery
of shags—cormorants
preening their white bellies,
floating the feathers free.

And those two tree trunks
snagged by the far bank
are motor-powered canoes,
churning the chill water
with their rotary roots.

Summer

The dead mussel shells are
miniature, hard-covered books
spread unread on the shore.

Waugal, Upper Swan

From any spot along the bank
you can see the spirit-snake
slip by—the Waugal,
the wakeful river's Dreaming.

It bucks above or skirts about
the rocks, slides by, gleaming,
each sud a white scale.
Watch all winter and you will

not see the end of its tail.
Yet come mid-summer
the serpent's flesh will rot away
leaving only a rubble of vertebrae.

Birth

Downhill from the herd,
a cow and her newborn calf.

The baby bull lies steaming
in a muddy puddle on the loam.

the cow nuzzles it,
rasps it roughly with her tongue.

A red rope of afterbirth
hangs in tandem with her tail.

Blood colours her urine.
Colostrum drips from her teats.

Wet and wonky, the calf
struggles to stand. Finally

on all fours, it wobbles
for a moment then collapses

as if a bullet had bludgeoned
its brain. Oh, this foreboding.

Four Men

The contraption is like a small
merry-go-round at a country fair:
five cradles at the end of five arms
which meet at a hub and turn

on an upright axle. Inverted
stirrups are welded to the sides
of each cradle. A man stands at,
and a lamb lies in, four of the cradles.

Four lambs on the merry-go-round.
The fourth man tosses one off. Spin
round. The first man lifts one up
and lays it on its back.

Much as a gynaecologist might
hook a woman's legs out and back,
he hooks the lamb's hocks
in the stirrups. Spin round.

The second man injects a poison
for parasites, jabbing the needle
in the sternum, and clips a piece
from an ear. No sound. Spin

round. The third man holds
a pair of sharp shears. He pinches
the fleece beside the tail
and snips. A crisp, fibrous sound,

like cutting cloth. It is an art
to cut no deeper than the depth
of the skin. Blood spurts out,
a thin jet, as from a water-pistol;

or, thinner yet, like a spray of juice
from an orange as it is peeled.
From the root of the tail, he cuts
along the side of the anus,

the vulva, skinning the lamb
alive. The exposed meat films
with blood. Barely a struggle.
Only a single, bleating scream

with the first cut. Mulesing,
they call it, and do it to safeguard
the flock from fly-strike.
Between the third man's boots,

shaped like a cow-pat, a pool-pile
of coagulating blood wobbles
like a jelly. Snip. Spin round.
The fourth man slips a rubber ring

on the tail. (With a ram lamb,
he clamps another ring around
the scrotum—that little purse
from which no ewe will ever receive

conception's shining currency.)
Then he unhooks the legs
and dumps the lamp in the dirt.
Spin round. Begin again. It takes

barely one minute. Mulesing.
I jot a few notes. The four men
are uneasy. What will the townie
write? 'Y'aren't an animal libber,

are ya?' Banter among the blood
and bleating. I concede there is
no mercy in a death by maggots.
The last lamb hobbles, bellowing,

to its mother, a red glare
at its rear. The pasture is splotched
with crimson. 'They've got their
tail-lights on,' the third man grins,

wiping the blood from his hands.

Cattle

I

A steer rubs its throat
on a steel picket: that discomfort
in the dewlap, close to the jugular.

II

Heifers stare at the auctioneer,
saliva drooling from their muzzles
like strings of silicone.

III

Nowhere to go, no one to follow,
a calf in the cattle yards
is hoisting its belly to bellow.

Smoko
(for John Korn)

Just half-way through
the jarrah log
the chainsaw chokes.

He jerks the blade
from the red wood.
As if at a joke

the old log grins.
From its mouth wafts
a wisp of smoke.

Idyll, Boyup Brook

The fields are green with clover;
ewes give suck to their lambs;
wood ducks graze with their ducklings;
and dabchicks dive in the dams.

Robins set fire to the roadside;
rosellas fly up from the oats;
kingfishers reel blue from the skyline;
and magpies toss tunes from their throats.

Shorn sheep line a creek like sandbags;
frogs rollick in the rushes and croak;
and among the trees in the orchard
almonds signal spring with white smoke.

I'd planned in the lines of my pastoral
to deny the encroachment of death:
the sheep are not trucked to the slaughter;
the birds are not robbed of their breath;

the frogs are safe from the heron;
the petals from the almonds don't fall.
But beauty in the end's an illusion,
an embroidery on the fringe of a pall.

So it's futile to think in the future
this poem will preserve what I saw
and readers will see the scene through me
unaware that I see it no more.

That Bird
(for Zenon Pirga)

Hiking in the Avon Valley
I saw a wedge-tailed eagle
circle like a bomber-plane
unsure of its target. It flapped

periodically to keep its height,
pumping the air between pauses.
Then suddenly it hit a thermal
and spiralled up, hanging

in the hammock of its wings.
Withough thought of me and
without my thought, the eagle
edged into and out of my vision.

That bird—so utterly other.
All day, it hung on the chain
of my thoughts like a crucifix.
In camp, I imagined it roosting

somewhere in the darkness,
blood on its talons, meat
in its gut. Like its prey,
it was bound for oblivion.

It was going into death without
knowing or being known. But by
this poem (imperfectly, temporarily)
I lift that bird above its destiny.

Jarrah

The calm of the forest amplifies
a faint, flat tintinnabulation.
The jarrah trees are just in bud
and the buds are beginning to burst.

Like miniature bracken fronds,
the filaments of each flower unfurl,
forcing open the operculum, the cap
that covers the nascent blossom.

As they fall, the floral caps
(small as the drum-stick heads
of matches) strike the dry leaf-
litter on the forest floor,

punctuate the stillness
with an arrhythmic percussion.
Like the particles of a sun shower,
they parachute at random

to the ground. One lands on the tip
of a blackboy leaf, balances
on the sharp leaf-shaft like
a bamboo hat on a lanky oriental.

Karri

That tree that thankfully is not
500 fence posts or 50 polished tables
or 20 bookcases crammed with books

—that tree that could be anything
(except alive) a skilled man
might sensibly conceive it to be

—that tree that stands in the air
like a condominium, crowned
with cranes and scaffolding

—*that* tree is unsettled by flowers,
those small plumes of white blossom
fluttering from the tonnes of wood.

Essentially, Eucalpytus

The Gungurru—*Eucalyptus caesia* Benth.—
more beautiful in flower than the Mottlecah,
the Rose of the West. Choose a blossom. It is

a red-headed golliwog; an unruly Ginger Meggs;
a fantasia light, yellow bursting
from the tips of a hundred red rods;

a feather duster powdered with pollen;
the nap on a motif on a Persian rug;
a scarlet tassel on the hem of a green robe;

a white-waisted ballerina in a bright tutu;
a coral-coloured sea anemone;
a sea urchin with tube feet but no spines.

These many marvellous things but
essentially this: a eucalyptus flower
with anthers of gold and filaments of fire.

Breaking Out

A eucalypt bud is an incarceration of strong men—
boxers—cramped, bent double in a green locker-room
with a conical ceiling-cum-roof. Though they dislike
each other, they co-operate, set their shoulders

to the shelter's cover. They press and push, crack
the seal that holds the ceiling to the circular wall,
then shunt the roof right off. Breaking out, they
cheer in bold colours, brandish their golden gloves.

Wind and Washing

The wind is a pack
of hounds, panting on the clothes-
line. They lick my face
with their lolling, linen tongues
as I peg the towels in place.

That Movement

Swishing the dish-water
to froth the detergent—that movement,
like ruffling a child's hair.

Trouser Legs

After the circus, dozens
of diminutive clowns on stilts
got slightly tipsy and tore

the drain-pipe trouser legs
from their pin-striped suits.
In defiance of council laws,

the thin, synthetic leggings
litter the public lawn
like plastic drinking straws.

Shift Focus
Hakea laurina

Naming is mostly metaphor. So with the Pincushion Hakea
the botanist pre-empted an image for flowers the poet
had yet to discover: blooms composed of stiff pistils pinned
in a scarlet cushion of compact petals. The bush, named
from the flower, named in turn from a correspondence.

Now shift focus to the fruit. The nut of the hakea
is a hard cocoon, a wooden chrysalis. Within, a pupa swells
on the plant's sap, matures into an indigo-black imago.
Fully winged, the butterfly bides its time, waiting
for drought or fire to crack the case for its release.

As a footprint through fossilisation leaves an imprint
in stone, so the imago in departure leaves an image
of wings—their perfect, candle-flame shapes—
on the paired planes of wood where the chrysalis gapes.

Native Pears

Unopened, the nuts of the native pear
are pale-green plumb-bobs.
They are the bodies of twig-necked ducks.
They are moulds for winged seeds.

As they dry to grey
stretch marks mar their Buddha bellies.

Opened, the nuts are
long-eared rabbits resting on their haunches.
They are wooden-winged butterflies.
They are castanets that cannot click.

Sandplain Sheoak

In the Boorabin National Park,
sprawl is the no-shape
of both scrub and shrub.

Yet in the minutiae of each,
many forms are defined.
Focus for this on the sheoak.

I

The leaves of the sand
plain sheoak are like pine
needles without a point.

And they are segmented
like the collapsible poles
of a hiker's tent.

II

Swelling at random, her flowers
cling in the middle of a stem
or in the cleft of branches like
pubic hair. Wispy, purple-pink,

they are hidden in the dark
not from prudery but from shame
that such a tuft of fluff
could take 'flower' for its name.

III

Prickly and compact,
her nuts are small echidnas
nestling in her bark,
suckling on her sap.

Snap one off and in a week
it becomes a termite nest:
flying ants emerge wing-first
from the widening cracks.

Drought

On a branch
of the dead hakea bush
a cluster of grey nuts:

a family of finches
huddled together,
beaks agape.

Into Darkness

I am walking at dusk in the lull
between rain. Slugs blot
the footpath. Faintly luminous,
flowers reflect the residual light.

I pass pink, loose-petalled roses,
clumped on bushes like soggy tissues,
and white cabbage chrysanthemums,
battered to the ground and spattered

with sand. I am breaching the border
of twilight, trying not to fear
the fate of my children as they face
the frontier. Like the planet,

my thoughts spin nightward. Retreating,
the day destroys the third dimension,
deprives the world of depth.
Trees turn black. In silhouette

a spindly eucalypt sculptures the rain,
its slender leaves flouncing
in squalls in the hesitant wind.
Through radiating tiers of branches

a Norfolk Island pine points the way
to heaven, holds highmost a cross.
I am walking into darkness. Colours
are draining away, shapes dissolving.

All the old certainties are lost.
Above, the moon is a spillage of light
mopped up by the clouds. The moon
with its meaning: the sun that shone

is still shining. I am walking
through the dark on the turning world.

After Reading a Newspaper

It's as if some of the ink
that smudges my fingers
has blackened my soul, too.

Against the Wall

In the garden against
the sandstone wall
of Fremantle Prison,
a guard's Siamese cat

is teasing a mouse.
Tail twitching, it cuffs
the small creature
across the patchy lawn,

sends it tumbling
like a grey leaf
struck by the wind.
Leaping in pursuit,

it cuffs the mouse
again—claws un-
sheathed, a tin bell
tinkling at its throat.

Sometimes in the Dark

There is, someone claims,
a pup in the prison.
And then a *yap*! confirms
it. Who now can work?

The women, the inmates,
are excited. The welfare
officer has passed the gates
with a pup at her heels!

It is trotting along
the verandah, towards
H Block—springy, strong
and defiantly doggy.

'Oh!' says one 'girl'
who is serving time
for murder. Memories whirl.
'Oh, I haven't seen a dog

for nearly four years!'
The bars are no barrier
to the pup. It peers
through and the murderess

picks it up and hugs
it with a hard urgency.
It licks her face. No drugs
could put that distance

in her eyes. She thinks,
Four years and six to go.
She shakes her head, blinks
and says for consolation:

'But sometimes in the dark
far off, I hear them bark.'

Sounding-board

I remember, when my brother died,
placing my wrist-watch face down
on a literary journal in which I
had a poem published and hearing
quite unexpectedly in the pre-
dawn stillness the hollow sound
of its ticking, as if the magazine
cover had become a sounding-board
to amplify the tongue of time,
the silence between the seconds.

Touch

When I touched him, the old man,
when I interrupted his struggle
to remember what he wanted
to say and said, 'Look

at the rainbow bird'—
when I touched his arm
the flesh was saggy, loose
like old canvas on a windless day.

I tried not to think of it.
I let go and said, 'Up there,
look.' It was on the high wire,
colourless against the clear sky.

No hint of iridescence,
no hues of rainbows, but
I recognised its shape—
the bullet body, the sharp beak,

the twin thin feathers
trailing from the tail.
He looked up, the old man
looked up and looked puzzled.

'I used to know all the names,'
he said. 'What did you call it?'
'A rainbow bird. They come down
from the Kimberleys to nest.'

'I love birds. I used to know
all the names. But now
I don't know any.' This horror.
The mind like the arm and

a greater slackness coming.
When I looked back, the bird
was gone. Only the wire
like a scratch on the perfect sky.

Civil Rights Poem for Christmas

Murder? I resent the implication!
It's *hardly* human. Take it
from me, I've done this before.
All you see is blood. Get rid
of it now. Who'd be the poorer?

What? Look, I frankly don't believe
that angel-spoke-to-me, Son-of-God
stuff. Nor will anyone else.
Everyone knows there's only one way . . .

Hold on! All right! I'm sorry.
Okay? I'm just trying to give you
some sensible advice. After all,
what are friends for? Look at it
like this . . . Uh! Hear me out.

The fact is, you're not married.
Think of the shame once you begin
to show. Think of Joseph. D'you
really believe he'll still want you?

And there's something else.
They could stone you—then it'd die
anyway. Think of yourself. What
of the future? And besides, what
sort of life will the little . . .?

Okay, Miss Very-so-Virgin! Get off
your Son-of-the-Most-High horse.
I'm just trying to help. One day
you'll regret not listening to reason.

Golgotha

Finally, one arrives at the place
of the skull because there is nowhere
else to go. And there before the face
of bone one pauses in despair.

The culmination of all evil
is displayed before one's eyes.
Man's heart conspired with the devil
and cared little for disguise.

Yet if, at the sight of the Cross,
a light is struck on the rough of the brain
and the mind conceives all bar this is vain,

There comes a voice that reassures. Thus
is the seed of tenderness sown
in the cleft of the heart of stone.

White Gum

This white-barked wandoo,
this most-Australian gum,
rises through the air, rigid
with wood, latent with post

and cross-beam. It is fitting,
really, that this eucalypt,
this kinstree to the Cross
of the Son of God, should be

an incarnation of the light
of the sun—the same sun
the world over, the millennia
long. Run your hand up the trunk

towards the limbs you cannot
reach. There are no splinters
in the bark. Go ahead, touch
the wood, the living timber

the nails have yet to pierce.

Bread

In the beginning God
made grain so that men
might make bread

so that every loaf
might proclaim
its archetype,

the Living Bread
come down from heaven.
Give thanks and eat!

Marri with Nuts

After rain
sometimes gumnuts
—the big-bowled,

boldly rimmed
nuts of the marri
—smoulder

as if packed
with tobacco
and set alight.

Or, which is
more beautiful,
as if each nut

were a thurible,
a wooden censer,
wafting incense.

Indeed, this
green-robed tree
is a thurifer

unconsciously
praising God
most consciously

through me.

Detection

Like most eucalypts,
the gungurru tree is
a *ra*dio *d*etection
*a*nd *r*anging installation.

Each flower is a radar
aerial—floral dish,
a parabolic reflector
camouflaged in red cordage;
pistil, a waveguide
pointing the boresight.

Each antenna targets
the roving eye,
transmits shape and colour
in continuous phase,
detects by reflection
the location of praise.

Communion

(for Iain and Liz Parker)

The garden is dry but the bird-bath
brims with black water from the bottom
of the dam. Beside the gravel path

two stumps beckon small birds from the bush,
invite with a voice they never had
when fused, infused with the sap's green push.

One, on its plane, bears sugar and grain.
The other, in a glazed clay dish, holds
the dark dregs of last winter's light rain.

A neat, white-naped honeyeater takes
a bath. A fantail alights to flirt.
On the flat grass nearby, like snow flakes,

a fall of rolled oats. Be still. Don't speak.
Share this communion: a blue wren is
breaking a white wafer with his beak.

Turtle-doves

Beneath the almond tree,
in constant close proximity
to each other, two Indian

turtle-doves quick
step nervously on the lawn.
They bob among the broken nut

shells, search for food
fragments fallen from the ripe
white kernels the king parrots

carelessly eat with their hawk
beaks and bean tongues. Some
times nature seems invigorated

by an inadvertent love—
as when the hooligan parrot
helps the immigrant dove.

Abundance
(for Tamah)

Standing on a flower-
basket hanging beside
the blue bird cage hooked on
a branch of the lemon

tree, a turtle-dove pokes
its head between the bars
to peck the seed spilt by
the wasteful budgerigars.

Heron in Sunlight

The heron whose shadow
is laid out
like a shroud
beneath the shallows

is unaware that

as it stands
it structures non-light
to the day's slope
and the body's shape.

Scale, plume, beak:

it stands in three
dimensions,
its doppelgänger
fixed to its feet.

Mongolian Dotterel, Moore River Estuary

Who knows what mystery stirs
the dotterel to our spring?
Hatching out in Siberia, it

quells death, quills wings, stores
strength, until at length, cuffed
by the coming cold, it climbs

the air's everwending stairs
that lead to all shores and none.
Leaving land for land, it flies

above the ocean's white-plumed
wings. At sea at night it steers
along the lit-up laneways

of heaven. How can this happen
if life's origin is Chance?
Evidence of Design stares

from the bird's journey and body
as brightly as the light
from the distant, burning stars.

Quatrains, Swan Valley

I Winter: Foam

It seems the egret roosting
on the rock in the river
is moulting, shedding white
feathers to the flowing water.

II Spring: Anticipation

Did I step on it or
merely startle it?—
the cicada screeching
in the shed leaves.

III Summer: Aspiration

This last aspiration:
as they die and dry
mussel shells hinge open
as if trying to fly.

IV Autumn: Loss

The wounds have healed.
And yet the leafless vines
look like rows of stitches
on the face of the field.

Barely Spring

With their out-
stretched branches
beginning to bud

the woody vines

are stocky girls
with green ribbons
in their plaits.

Willow

The willow is a fisherman,
and highly successful at that.
I refer not to the rods
it rests towards the river
in winter, but to the strings
of fish it shoulders in summer.
The tree teems with fish—
small, green minnows strung
by their heads, dangling
one below the other, some
twisting in the dry breeze.

Tree-fern

The tree-fern is an orchestra
playing a pastorale. Glorious
the meticulous melodies, the green
movements. On centre stage
the soloist lifts his violin—
light on the line of the neck,
the tuning pegs, the perfect
carved curl—poised to begin.

Hostilities

Those banana trees
are an Indian war-party
armed with feathered lances.

Agitated, the braves
shake their weapons,
make the green feathers

flutter along the shafts.

Maize Metamorphosis

Though it may seem
amazing, most maize
plants become poultry
by summer's end.

A stand of sweet
corn, when it's
dry as a shock,
becomes a flock

of leghorn hens.
They're shy, don't
like to be seen,
but turn your back

and you'll learn
what I mean.
Listen. Already
they're scratching

about for greens.
And did you note
how they wait—
simply won't

begin to fossick—
until the wind
wields its trowel
to smooth the sound

of their work?
Och! The furtive fowl!
How could they have
learnt such a lurk?

Sunflower

The sunflower, evolutionists
will be elated to learn,
is in the process of becoming

an enormous insect. Vegetable
to animal—a veritable
missing link! The sunflower.

It is an almost-blowfly
watching the wondrous world
through a compound eye.

Almond

The almond tree about mid-autumn becomes
(wait—savour it!) a Rhode Island rooster,
feathered in russets and reds.

It struts in its season about the backyard
bestowing feathers on lawn and flowerbed,
displaying its finery to the ever-green lemon.

When the wind, that old fox, is on the prowl
the conceited cock flaps and crows, all
puffed up with bravado and banter.

It spars at the air with its twiggy spurs.
The coxcomb! Inevitably, I wake near winter
to find the fox has taken it by the throat

and shaken its feathers off. But I'm not
alarmed. For the almond is a phoenix fowl,
replenishing its plumes each spring.

Leaf and Load

The rain is breaking its phials
on the ornamental plum. From
the verandah I choose a leaf,

glistening with wet, and watch
until each vein becomes a rill
running into the midrib-river

and on to the leaf's tip
where the waters gather in a blister
to weight the leaf downwards

by imperceptible degrees. Slipping
from the chlorophyll plane, the rain-
drop hangs from the leaf-tip

as a ball-bearing might hang
from the point of a magnet, held
by the barest contact between

curve and cusp. Like a miniature,
transparent balloon tied by a child
to a tap, the drop swells,

bulges with a fragile elasticity,
bowing the leaf with its growing load,
until loosed at last by gravity.

Released, the leaf leaps up,
shudders to an easy equilibrium
in the light, impacting rain.

Five Haiku

I

Like catching a crab
in spawn—lifting a fern frond,
the spores spotted there.

II

Norfolk Island pine:
a ziggurat without walls
between the terraces.

III

The strelitzia:
a bright origami bird
of paradise. Peck.

IV

The frangipani,
two dimensional at dusk:
a many-headed hydra.

V

Hibiscus blossom,
lambent in the last light. Dark
shapes. Hawaiian girls . . .

Fodder
(for Stephen and Murray)

My son and his friend are gathering flowers
from the hibiscus bush that reaches over
the pickets that plot our neighbour's yard.
I watch them, these ten-year-old boys,
intrigued by their sudden interest
in horticulture. The old bush rests
its rods on the ridge of the fence,
and like fish the boys leap up to snatch
the bright lures. Finally, their dish full
of double-petalled blossoms, they stroll
to the rabbit hutch. I visualise
the red petals against the white fur.

Chook and Children

It never recovered from motherhood, the black hen.
It went clucky, hoarded eggs, hatched chickens
and turned vicious. Months later and still
it fluffs to a fury and hurls itself at our legs.

A plump, feathered lance, it draws blood
from our fatted calves. The children are afraid
to collect the eggs. Terror roams the chook-run.
Today, it hurtled at my son as he reached

into the feed-bin. He fended it off with the lid,
held like a shield at his shins, until I arrived
with a tomato stake to beat it back. It baulked,
squawked and flapped a swift retreat. The children

rejoice. Oh-ho, father with justice in his fist!
Ah-ha, the chicken-livered chook! Under the apple
tree the fowl fluffs up, shakes off its fright.
Looking on, my daughter says, 'Deserves him right!'

Family

'There's no one as good as us,
is there Mum?' my grandmother said
my mother said when she was young.
So, without forethought or fuss,

she defined, as only children can,
her family and herself : familiar
with the lineaments of love, she felt
at home in her home. As a man

I hear her speak, this woman who
was once a girl my father never
knew. My mother, in all her grief
and grace. As if they were new

she remembers the old sureties
and shares them now with me—
this woman whom I love because
like Christ she first loved me.

Mother, oh! be assured of this:
what is true for you is true for me
(and may my children say the same),
'There's no one, not one as good as us!'

Learning the Language

CTA. How am I able to write
even this? For, in the beginning,
there is a supposition that I know
the letters and their correlation
by the rules of language to 'it'.
TCA. 'It' is in my children's sandpit
scratching a hole for 'its' excrement.
ATC? This is a question of excellence.
A partaking of a perfection. WAAAOW!
my daughter squeals, finding her sound
to signify the thing whose existence
excites her. We mimic her, charmed
by her childishness. Were she older,
it would be grotesque, this word-
lessness. TAC. 'It' squats in the sand,
tail twitching. Our language—has it
no objective reality? Are standards
in literacy and literature really
illusory, elitist? ACT. *Scat!*
'It' leaps from the sandpit, scrabbles
over the picket fence. (How can I say
these things, how can you receive them,
if not in obedience to something Other?)
WAAAOW! Soon my daughter will conform
to the conventions that will liberate
her into speech. She will learn most
excellently to say, Pussy. CAT.

Five Tanka
(for Naomi, aged three)

I

'I heard a song and
it was pink,' she says, pestering
me to come and see.
I follow her to the front yard
as the ice-cream van drives away.

II

'He thought I was lettuce,'
she says, stroking the rabbit
that bit her. It nestles
in her lap—the little rodent
that her brother named 'White Fang'.

III

'We saw a different
owl with a big, big, long beak.'
Grandma is impressed.
Such things at the zoo! Mother
says, 'She means a pelican'.

IV

'Is the moon having
babies when it's fatter?' 'No,'
I say. We're driving
home. The night holds a full moon.
She says, 'Well sometimes moons do!'

V

'Do Kookeeburras
eat cookies?' she asks. The bird
laughs again, rattling
it out. We are bush-walking.
She holds my hand, my heart.

Frog
(for Tamah)

'Hear that frog?' my daughter
asks. I listen. 'Where?'
'That burping sound.
Right in the garden there.'

She brushes a bush. Abruptly,
as if she had touched
the pendulum of a clock,
the cicada stops tocking.

That's Fish

Say 'Quark!' they say,
my daughters.

I comply.
And quick as casual

quoit players
they flick

their hands at me.
Inexplicable!

'That's fish,'
the elder explains.

Father, poet, pelican:
I am hungry

with happiness.
'Quark!'

They toss more
invisible fish.

The Grasshopper Heart

That man with the cowboy hat and tan and tattoos
is holding his little white-skinned daughter
very gently in the shallow water. Now he is
zooming her along, but not too quickly
for fear of her fear. He tosses her up,
catches and hugs her, holds in check
the fierce tenderness that craves to crush her.
Her father. His wholly holy love. He is smiling
and I know his heart is like a grasshopper—
leaping and landing spring-loaded to leap again.

Two Rivers

As they join, the Swan and Helena are hemmed
with a patchwork of paddocks and parks
where, in spring, birds come to court and mate.

Black ducks and moorhens navigate and nest
among reeds and bulrushes. Kingfishers
and parrots covet holes in river gums.

Honeyeaters and thornbills twist grass
and fluff among twigs and foliage. The fields
bloom with song. Even the drabbest birds

strew bright flowers from their throats.
Beneath the paperbarks, arum lilies
gather in their white habits like nuns

released from the convent of winter. And
bracken ferns raise their crosiers
to bless the opulent earth. People also

come. At King's Meadow Oval and Point Reserve
they plot the ground with picnic blankets
(radish red, broccoli blue, zucchini green)

like market gardeners growing happiness.
Men slap meat on barbecues; women rummage
through baskets; children bask on banks or

jump from jetties. And occasionally, with their
long leotard-white feet, canoeists perform
spurting *pas glisses* on the polished water.

Spring, Alfred Cove

This wildlife sanctuary: the last wetland on the Swan
River estuary. How long will it last? Some call it
wasteland, and few notice it at all. A patch of sedge

signals in semaphore to an inattentive world.
Samphires mat the mud-flats, their bulbous stems
like strings of red and green rosary beads. Bulrushes

grow on a bank, their cylindrical bales of wool
bursting open from the season's rough, ripe handling.
With its numerous, invisible needles, the wind

knits the water plain and purled. Pelicans,
their wings unfurled, float fathoms above the cove,
caught in slow, wide eddies. Terns in turn

kamikaze the battleship-grey water, rise again
unhurt. A dozen black ducks at the water's edge
quack quietly as they dredge the sludge. Stilts

step on their reflections with their spindly,
backward-bending legs. Cormorants practise tai chi
on wireless and weathered fence posts. An egret

stands without a mate beside a beached boat.
Also alone, a greenshank hunts along the sand-bars.
Soon others will come from Siberia,

charting their way by the changeless stars.

A Good Night

The mulies are in the harbour,
shoals of them, teeming unseen
in the opaque sea. On the wharf,

in rubber boots and yellow raincoats,
a team of professional fishermen
lure the fish with food and light.

They have hung a lantern, hissing
incessant warning, just above
the quilted surface of the quiet water;

and they have strewn pollard—
the pollen grains, the yeasty smell—
on the water, below the lamp,

above the submerged net—an iron hoop
looped with mesh, long and tapering
like a wind-sock. Near the net,

a ship shifts uneasily. Its rope,
a catenary from prow to bollard,
strains and straightens. Bilge-water

spouts from the hull. On the wharf,
an enormous, enclosed conveyor-belt
rolls on its gantry. Grain

cascades into the hold. Behind
the ship, winnowed by the wind
and stretching as far as the shining

of the harbour lights, barley husks
form a yellow slick on the black
water. Between the lamp and the net

the mulies, the bait-fish, swirl
like long-bodied moths. At a command,
the men hoist the net. It is a crucible

bubbling with molten silver.
Poured out, the fish separate
into small, oblong ingots. A young man

smooths them into shallow crates,
ready for freezing. But the fish
are not ready. Frenzied,

they flick and twist, scales flying off
like sequins from a silver purse.
Their gills gape, the red frills

clogged by air. Their mouths gasp,
transparent lips extended
like trumpets, blaring, 'O! O!'

The conveyor-belt and the bilge-pump
drone a duet to drown Death's reveille.
The ship's rope heaves and relaxes.

In a child's hand, a line twitches
like a caught nerve. In the crates,
the fish have gone off the boil

and lay eternally still. The men
lower the net again. 'Gonna be a good
night,' smiles one man, his hair

spangled with scales, like confetti.

From the Midnight Courtyard

ELIZABETH RIDDELL

Elizabeth Riddell has not been a prolific poet, but the poems of her smallish oeuvre have often stayed with readers for decades. Several are already essential parts of the Australian literary heritage. Raised in New Zealand, long resident in Australia, she is always a distinctive writer, her poems continually achieving fresh approaches as they move back and forth across the Tasman. Carefully chosen and arranged by the poet herself, in an order which, rather than merely chronological, is in fact intrinsic to her writing and its inner life, this book distils the work of a lifetime, and restores to readers a wealth of fine-grained achievement.

Years Found in Likeness

ALAN GOULD

Alan Gould's abiding concern with time and with the historical moment of human lives has never found richer, freer or more musical expression than in this new book of his verse. The book is, as ever, full of deep insight and arresting surprise. A delightful physicality and crispness inhere in the sequence of Monaro poems, blue with skies, mountain flowers and snow – and the blue note is modulated hilariously in the last poem of that section. The largest component of the collection, however, is a moving and splendidly paced libretto specially written for Graham Hair's choral symphony *The Great Circle* which, commemorating Cook's voyages to the Pacific, sums up and brings to a natural culmination the poet's other great themes of ships, the oceans and planetary life.

Sixty

John Rowland

John Rowland seems to have been invigorated by his return home from senior diplomatic life abroad. A meditative poet of privacies, of old gardens and windy uplands, his nature writing in this collection is especially fine, and his mature contemplation of age in the poems from which the book takes its title is deeply moving. Also, in this book he brings to a personal crux the old tension between Australian newness and European depth of culture. In this, as in its measured lucidity, his verse belongs in a central tradition of Australian writing. The late Kenneth Slessor wrote of Rowland's first book: 'His poems have elegance, wit, cool observation and a genuine sense of beauty and wonder.'

Selected Poems

Eric Rolls

Eric Rolls was born in Grenfell in 1923. He has been involved with the land for most of his life and believes that 'the soil is the perfect background for a writer'. Until 1986 he farmed full-time at Cumberdeen, Baradine, where he still lives and where he has written most of his award-winning histories, including *They All Ran Wild* and *A Million Wild Acres*, and celebrations of Australian life.

Selected Poems, drawn from two previously published volumes and occasional publishing over more than fifty years, demonstrates his gift for nature lyrics as well as satire and irony.

Selected Poems

ROBERT GRAY

'As an imagist, he is without a rival in the English-speaking world.'
Kevin Hart, SYDNEY MORNING HERALD

An earlier edition of this book won the National Poetry Award at the Adelaide Arts Festival, the New South Wales Premier's Award and the Grace Leven Prize, and was described as the work of 'a major Australian poet'.

For this printing of one of the best-selling volumes in the A&R Modern Poets series, the author has further revised a number of his poems, and has included the entire content of his most recent book, *Piano*.

Collected Poems

DAVID CAMPBELL

David Campbell was born at Ellerslie, Adelong, New South Wales, in 1915 and died in 1979. With his wide range and sureness of touch, he is regarded as one of Australia's finest poets. This collected edition compiled by Leonie Kramer includes all the poems from his individual volumes published between 1949 and 1979, with the exception of the translations of Russian poetry, and some previously uncollected poems.

Selected Poems

GWEN HARWOOD

Gwen Harwood was born in Brisbane in 1920. Keenly interested in music, she was to teach music and serve for a time as organist at All Saints' Church, Brisbane. Married with four children, she is now a grandmother and pursues many interests including the study of modern philosophy and working with composers.

This revised edition of *Selected Poems* incorporates her acclaimed collection, *Bone Scan*, which won the 1989 Victorian Premier's Literary Award for poetry. Other awards received by Gwen Harwood include the Grace Levin Prize 1975, the Robert Frost Award 1977 and the Patrick White Award 1978. In 1988 she received an Honorary Doctorate of Letters from the University of Tasmania.

The Earthquake Lands

HAL COLEBATCH

'A genuine poet... here is the true rebel of the 1980s.'
C.J. Koch, SYDNEY MORNING HERALD

The Earthquake Lands, Hal Colebatch's fourth volume, is a poetry of satire and celebration, anger and hope. While his world can be peopled with monsters, it is also filled with beauty and delight and a sense of the wonder of things. This is the poetry of post-modern man, facing the future with both optimism and fear, yet acutely aware of the heritage of the past and the unity of human experience. It celebrates human heroism and the natural world, its celebration sometimes offset by savage indignation.

Hal Colebatch is a poet of unconventional hope, courageously working to break poetry out of its twentieth-century ghetto, so as to reach again the wide audience it has had in other ages.